Lute music by Nicolaus Schmall von Lebendorf for CGDA Mandola

Ondřej Šárek

Contents

Introduction	3
How to read tablature	3
Dimmi Amore	4
Courante	6
Saltarella	8
Balleto	10
Bergamesca	11
Intrada Anglica	11
Corrente	12
Englesa	13
Galliarda	14
Chorea I.	15
Nachtanz I.	15
Chorea II.	16
Nachtanz II.	16
Chorea III.	17
Nachtanz III.	18
Chorea IV.	19
Nachtanz IV.	20
Chorea V.	21
Nachtanz V.	22
Intrada I.	23
Intrada II.	24
Kindlein	25

Copyright © 2020 Ondřej Šárek
All rights reserved.
ISBN: 9798609754264
Imprint: Independently published

Introduction

In this book you will find 22 short compositions by Baroque composer and lute player Nicolaus Schmall von Lebendorf. Sometimes his name is written in Czech form Mikuláš Šmal from Lebendorf.
It is not known so much about his life. It was founded that he lived around 1600 and worked as a scribe at Prague Castle.
Nice moments with songs that are interesting for melody and harmony.

How to read tablature

Score

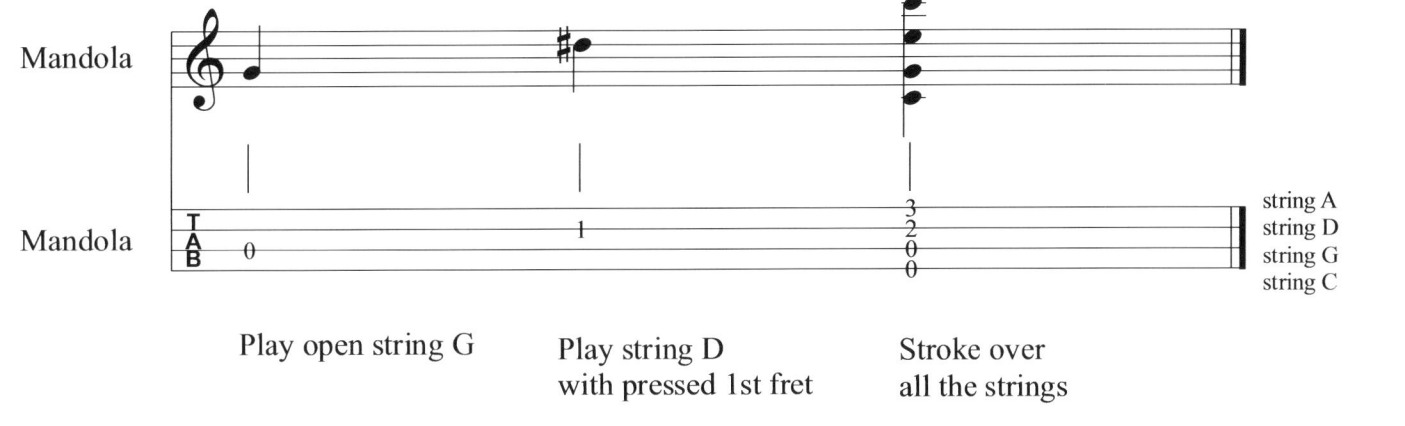

Mandola

Mandola

string A
string D
string G
string C

Play open string G

Play string D
with pressed 1st fret

Stroke over
all the strings

3 Copyright © 2020 Ondřej Šárek

Dimmi Amore

Music: N. Schmall von Lebendorf (cca 1600)
arr: Ondřej Šárek

Score
Mandola

4 Copyright © 2020 Ondřej Šárek

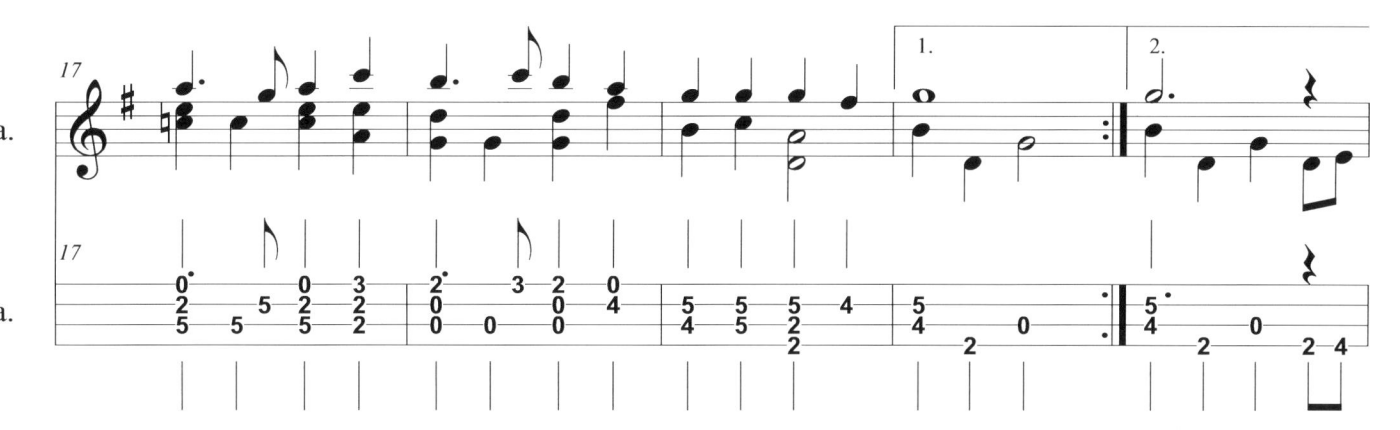

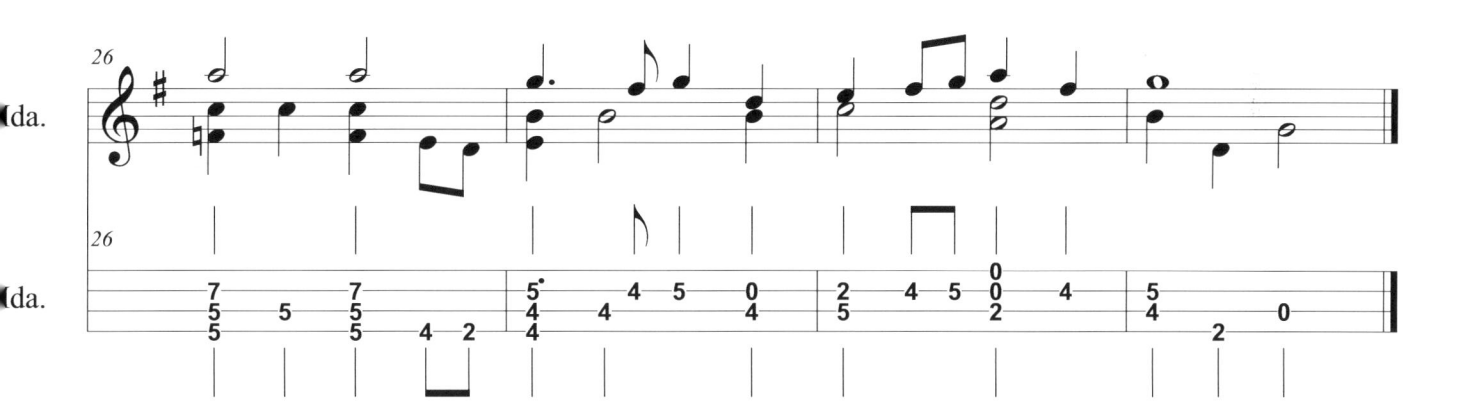

Dimmi Amore

Courante

Music: N. Schmall von Lebendorf (cca 1600)
arr: Ondřej Šárek

Copyright © 2020 Ondřej Šárek

Courante

Saltarella

Music: N. Schmall von Lebendorf (cca 1600)
arr: Ondřej Šárek

Saltarella

Balleto

Music: N. Schmall von Lebendorf (cca 1600)
arr: Ondřej Šárek

10 Copyright © 2020 Ondřej Šárek

Bergamesca

Music: N. Schmall von Lebendorf (cca 1600)

arr: Ondřej Šárek

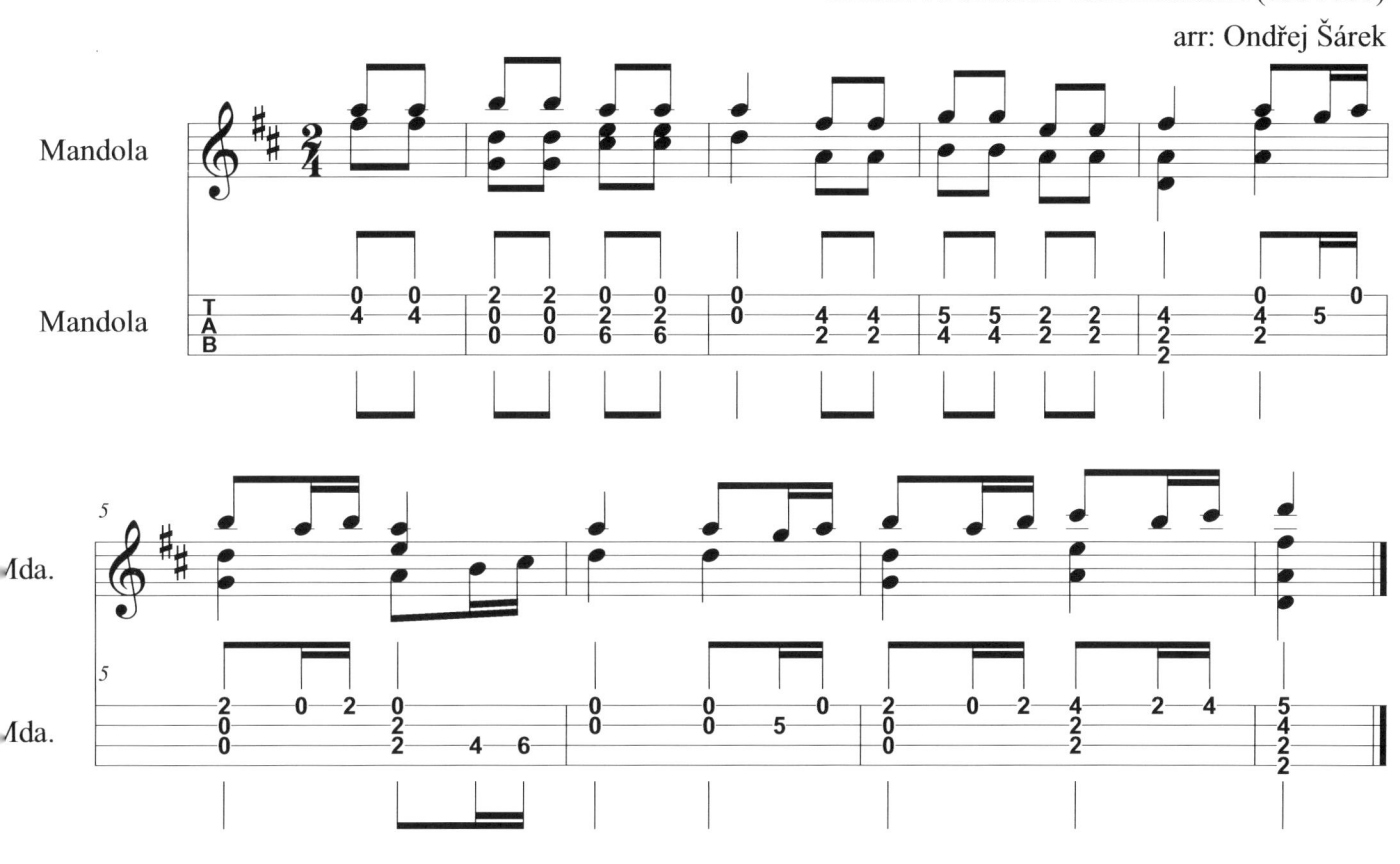

Intrada Anglica

Music: N. Schmall von Lebendorf (cca 1600)

arr: Ondřej Šárek

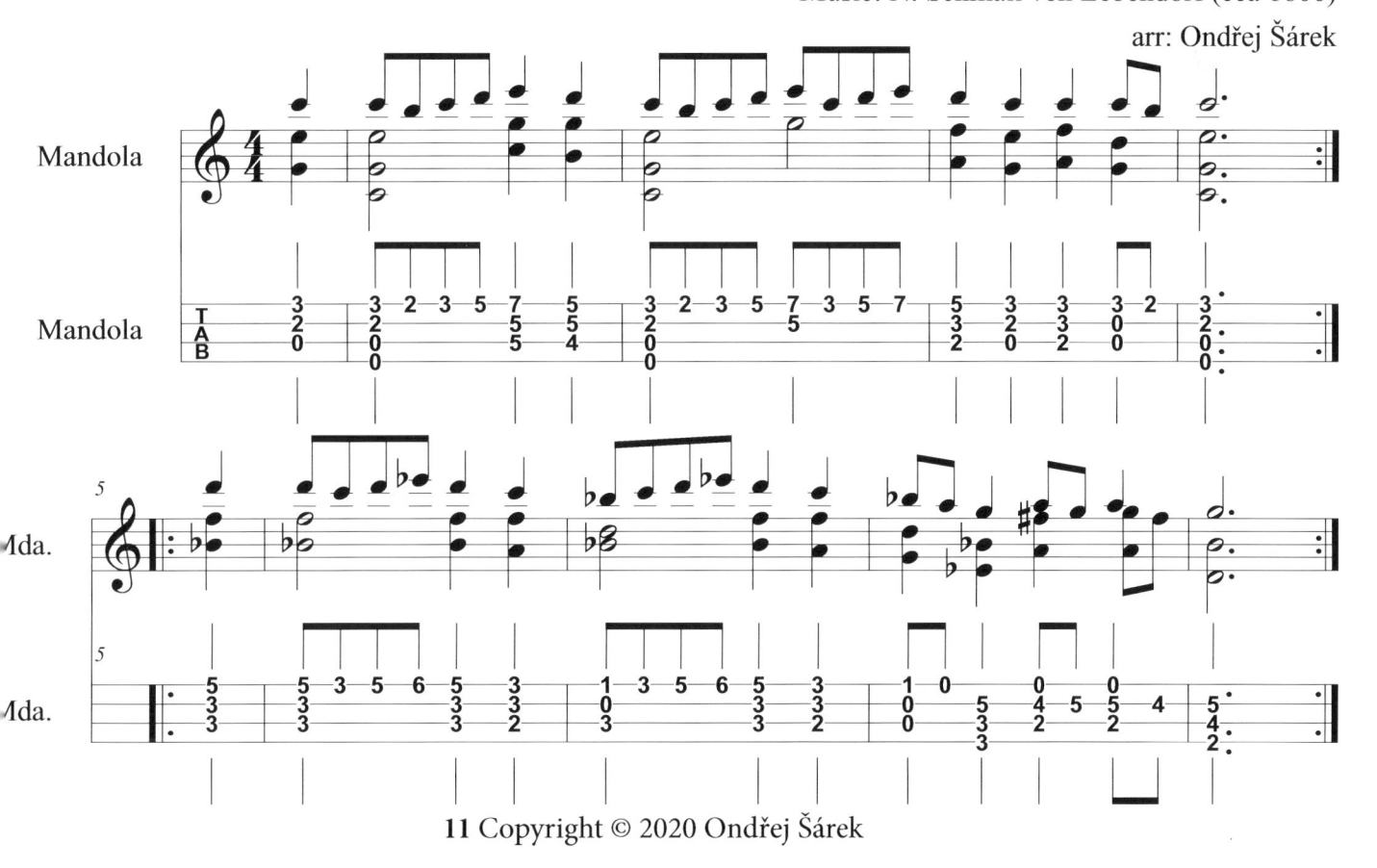

Corrente

Music: N. Schmall von Lebendorf (cca 1600)
arr: Ondřej Šárek

Englesa

Music: N. Schmall von Lebendorf (cca 1600)

arr: Ondřej Šárek

Galliarda

Music: N. Schmall von Lebendorf (cca 1600)

arr: Ondřej Šárek

14 Copyright © 2020 Ondřej Šárek

Chorea I.

Music: N. Schmall von Lebendorf (cca 1600)
arr: Ondřej Šárek

Nachtanz I.

Music: N. Schmall von Lebendorf (cca 1600)
arr: Ondřej Šárek

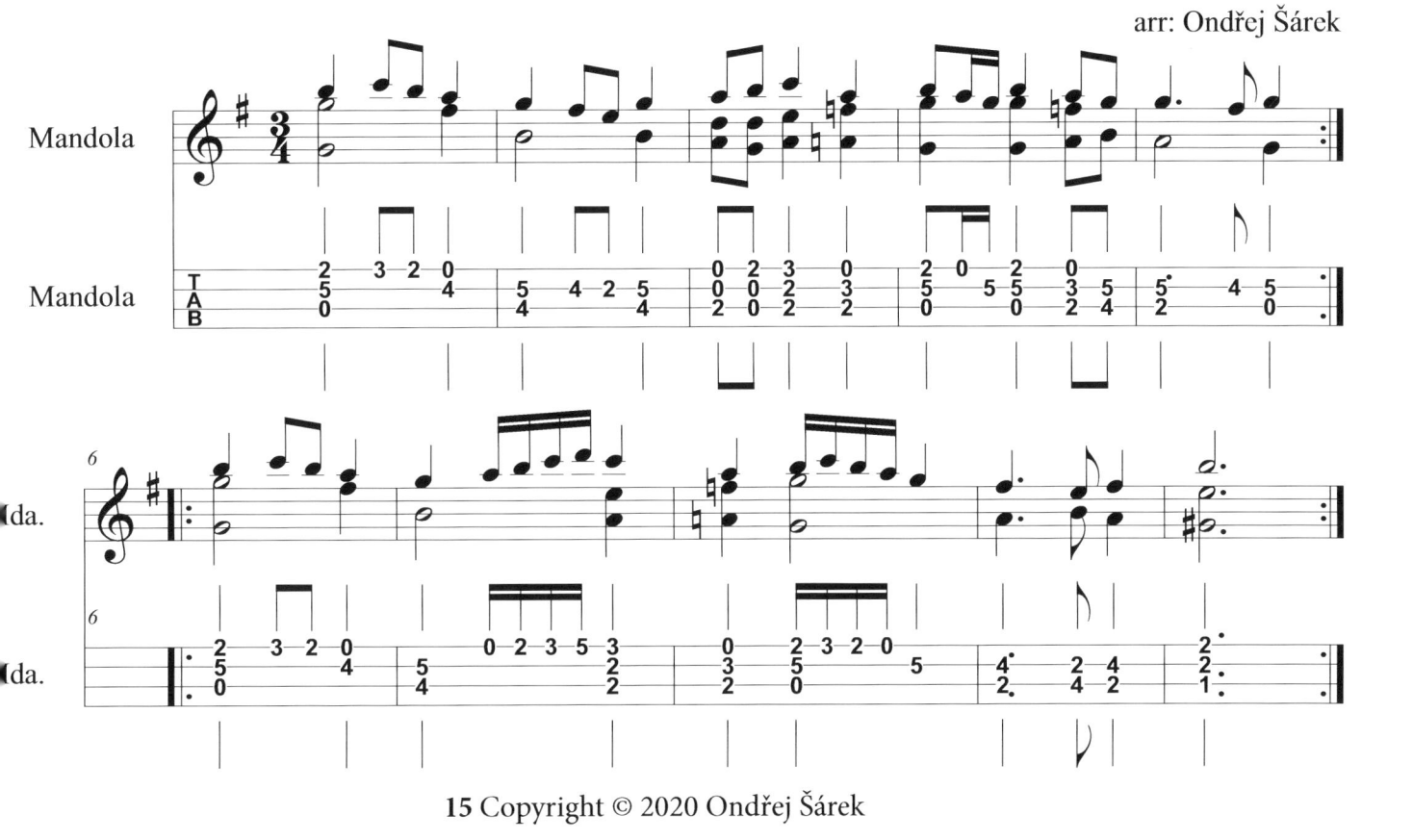

Chorea II.

Music: N. Schmall von Lebendorf (cca 1600)
arr: Ondřej Šárek

Nachtanz II.

Music: N. Schmall von Lebendorf (cca 1600)
arr: Ondřej Šárek

Chorea III.

Music: N. Schmall von Lebendorf (cca 1600)

arr: Ondřej Šárek

Nachtanz III.

Music: N. Schmall von Lebendorf (cca 1600)

arr: Ondřej Šárek

Chorea IV.

Music: N. Schmall von Lebendorf (cca 1600)
arr: Ondřej Šárek

Nachtanz IV.

Music: N. Schmall von Lebendorf (cca 1600)

arr: Ondřej Šárek

Chorea V.

Music: N. Schmall von Lebendorf (cca 1600)
arr: Ondřej Šárek

Nachtanz V.

Music: N. Schmall von Lebendorf (cca 1600)
arr: Ondřej Šárek

22 Copyright © 2020 Ondřej Šárek

Intrada I.

Music: Nicolaus Schmall von Lebendorf (cca 1600)
arr: Ondřej Šárek

Intrada II.

Music: N. Schmall von Lebendorf (cca 1600)
arr: Ondřej Šárek

Kindlein

Music: N. Schmall von Lebendorf (cca 1600)

arr: Ondřej Šárek

Mandolin
Czech Medieval Mandolin
Gregorian chant for flatpicking Mandolin
Czech Renaissance folk songs for Mandolin
Classical music for Mandolin volume 1
Christmas Carols for Crosspicking Mandolin *volume 1*
Robert Burns songs for Mandolin
Compositions for Mandolin
18 Dance Tunes from Caslav Region for Mandolin
Fingerpicking Mandolin or GDAE Ukulele Solo
Notebook for Anna Magdalena Bach and Fingerpicking Mandolin or GDAE Ukulele
10 songs from the years 1899-1920 for Mandolin
Czech Hymnbook for Mandolin
Boogie woogie patterns for Mandolin
Jewish songs for Mandolin
Songs from old Prague for Mandolin
Carols from the world for Mandolin
Lute music by Nicolaus Schmall von Lebendorf for Mandolin

Duet for Mandolin and other instrument
Notebook for Anna Magdalena Bach for Mandolin and EADGBE Guitar
Notebook for Anna Magdalena Bach for Mandolin and instrument from the mandolin family
Notebook for Wolfgang for Mandolin and EADGBE Guitar
Notebook for Wolfgang for Mandolin and instrument from the mandolin family

Irish (GDAD) Bouzouki
Christmas Carols for Crosspicking GDAD Bouzouki volume 1
Classical music for GDAD Bouzouki volume 1
Czech Renaissance folk songs for GDAD Bouzouki
Josef Pekárek *Two Hanakian operas* for GDAD Bouzouki
Robert Burns songs for GDAD Bouzouki
18 Dance Tunes from Caslav Region for GDAD Bouzouki
Gregorian chant for GDAD Bouzouki
Compositions for GDAD Bouzouki
Gospel GDAD Bouzouki Solos
10 songs from the years 1899-1920 for GDAD Bouzouki
Czech Hymnbook for GDAD Bouzouki
Boogie woogie patterns for GDAD Bouzouki
Jewish songs for GDAD Bouzouki
Songs from old Prague for GDAD Bouzouki
Gospel for Fingerpicking GDAD Bouzouki
Czech Hymnbook for Fingerpicking GDAD Bouzouki
Carols from the world for GDAD Bouzouki
Lute music by Nicolaus Schmall von Lebendorf for GDAD Bouzouki

Mandola or Tenor Banjo or Tenor Guitar (CGDA)
Classical music for Mandola or Tenor Banjo volume 1
18 Dance Tunes from Caslav Region for Mandola or Tenor Banjo
Robert Burns songs for Mandola or Tenor Banjo
Gregorian chant for Mandola or Tenor Banjo
Fingerpicking Mandola or Tenor Banjo
10 songs from the years 1899-1920 for CGDA Mandola
Czech Hymnbook for CGDA Mandola
Boogie woogie patterns for CGDA Mandola
Christmas Carols for Crosspicking Mandola or Tenor Banjo
Compositions for CGDA Mandola
Romantic Pieces by František Max Kníže for fingerpicking CGDA Tenor Guitar
Classical music for fingerpicking CGDA Tenor Guitar
Cut capo for CGDA tenor banjo or guitar: First touch
Cut capo 2220 for CGDA tenor banjo, tenor guitar or mandola
Cut capo 2002 for CGDA tenor banjo, tenor guitar or mandola
Czech Hymnbook for fingerpicking CGDA Tenor Guitar
Czech Renaissance folk songs for CGDA Mandola or Tenor Banjo
Jewish songs for CGDA Mandola or Tenor Banjo
Songs from old Prague for CGDA Mandola or Tenor Banjo
Irish tunes for CGBD Tenor Banjo or Tenor Guitar
Carols from the world for CGDA Tenor Banjo or Mandola
Lute music by Nicolaus Schmall von Lebendorf for CGDA Mandola

G tuning (gDGBD) Banjo
Czech Medieval G tuning Banjo
Classical music for Clawhammer G tuning Banjo *volume 1*
Gregorian chant for G tuning Banjo
18 popular Czech Minuet for G tuning Banjo
Notebook for Anna Magdalena Bach and G tuning Banjo
18 Dance Tunes from Caslav Region for G tuning Banjo
Gospel for G tuning 5-string banjo
Jewish songs for G tuning 5-string banjo
Songs from old Prague for G tuning 5-string banjo
Carols from the world for G tuning 5-string banjo
Romantic Pieces by František Max Kníže for G tuning 5-string banjo

Plectrum (CGBD) Banjo
Gospel for CGBD Plectrum Banjo
Irish tunes for CGBD Plectrum Banjo
Robert Burns songs for CGBD Plectrum Banjo
18 Dance Tunes from Caslav Region for CGBD Plectrum Banjo
Notebook for Anna Magdalena Bach and CGBD Plectrum Banjo
Gregorian chant for CGBD Plectrum Banjo
Songs from old Prague for CGBD Plectrum Banjo
Czech Renaissance folk songs for CGBD Plectrum Banjo
Jewish songs for CGBD Plectrum Banjo
Carols from the world for CGBD Plectrum Banjo

DADGAD Guitar
Czech Medieval DADGAD Guitar
The canons for DADGAD Guitar
Fingerpicking DADGAD Guitar Solo
The Czech Lute for DADGAD Guitar
Gregorian chant for DADGAD Guitar
Gregorian chant for flatpicking DADGAD Guitar
Gospel DADGAD Guitar Solos
Notebook for Anna Magdalena Bach and DADGAD Guitar
Czech Renaissance folk songs for DADGAD Guitar
Robert Burns songs for DADGAD Guitar

EADEAE Guitar
Fingerpicking EADEAE Guitar Solo

CGDGCD (Orkney tuning) Guitar
Gospel CGDGCD Guitar Solos
Notebook for Anna Magdalena Bach and CGDGCD Guitar
Gregorian chant for flatpicking CGDGCD Guitar
Fingerpicking CGDGCD Guitar Solo

EADGBE Guitar
Czech Medieval EADGBE Guitar
Gregorian chant for flatpicking EADGBE Guitar
The canons for EADGBE Guitar
The Czech Lute for EADGBE Guitar
Czech Renaissance folk songs for EADGBE Guitar
Robert Burns songs for EADGBE Guitar
18 Dance Tunes from Caslav Region for EADGBE Guitar
Czech Hymnbook for EADGBE Guitar
18 popular Czech Minuet for EADGBE Guitar
Songs from old Prague for EADGBE Guitar

DADGBD (Double drop D tuning) Guitar
Gospel Double drop D tuning Guitar Solos
Notebook for Anna Magdalena Bach and Double drop D tuning Guitar

DADGBE (Drop D tuning) Guitar
Gospel Drop D tuning Guitar Solos
Notebook for Anna Magdalena Bach and Drop D tuning Guitar
Fingerpicking Drop D tuning Guitar Solo
Gregorian chant for flatpicking Drop D tuning Guitar
Robert Burns songs for Drop D tuning Guitar

Cut Capo (Partial Capo) Guitar
Cut capo flatpicking guitar songbook Gospel and Hymns I. II.
Cut capo flatpicking guitar songbook Christmas Carols
Cut capo flatpicking guitar songbook Jewish songs
Cut capo flatpicking guitar songbook Gregorian chant
Cut capo flatpicking guitar songbook Children's Songs

Guitalele (Guitarlele)
Fingerpicking Guitalele Solo volume I. II. III. IV. V.
Gregorian chant for Guitalele
The Czech Lute for Guitalele
Irish tunes for Guitalele
The canons for Guitalele
Gospel Guitalele Solos
Czech Medieval Guitalele
Czech Renaissance folk songs for Guitalele
Robert Burns songs for Guitalele
18 Dance Tunes from Caslav Region for Guitalele
Czech Hymnbook for Guitalele
18 popular Czech Minuet for Guitalele

Tres Cubano
traditionally tuned g4 g3 - c4 c4 - e4 e3
Gospel for Tres Cubano
Songbooks for Tres Cubano *volume 1., 2.*
Jewish songs for Tres Cubano

Tres Cubano
traditionally tuned g4 g3 - c4 c4 - e4 e3
split-string stroke
Tres Cubano Big Songbook
Gregorian chant for Tres Cubano
Songs from old Prague for Tres Cubano
Carols from the world for Tres Cubano

DAD Seagull Merlin
Czech Hymnbook for DAD Seagull Merlin
Robert Burns songs for DAD Seagull Merlin
Gospel for DAD Seagull Merlin
Jewish songs for DAD Seagull Merlin
Gregorian chant for DAD Seagull Merlin
Irish tunes for DAD Seagull Merlin
DAD Seagull Merlin Big Songbook
Carols from the world forDAD Seagull Merlin

New Ukulele books

For C tuning ukulele
Classics for Ukulele (MB)
Ukulele Bluegrass Solos (MB)
Antonin Dvorak: Biblical Songs
Irish tunes for all ukulele
Gospel Ukulele Solos
Gregorian chant for Ukulele
The Czech Lute for Ukulele
Romantic Pieces by Frantisek Max Knize for Ukulele
Notebook for Anna Magdalena Bach and Ukulele
Open Tunings for Ukulel (MB)
Robert Burns songs for ukulele
Jewish songs for C tuning ukulele
Campanella style songbook for beginner: C tuning ukulele
Antonín Dvořák: opera The Jacobin for ukulele
Leopold Mozart's Notebook for Wolfgang Arranged for Ukulele (MB)
The canons for one or two ukuleles
Solo and Variations for ukulele volume 1., 2., 3.
Czech Medieval Ukulele
Christmas Carols for ukulele
Harmonics for ukulele
43 Ghiribizzi by Niccolo Paganini for Ukulele
Christmas Carols for Clawhammer ukulele
Gospel Clawhammer ukulele Solos
Czech Renaissance folk songs for Ukulele
Classical music for Clawhammer Ukulele
Christmas Carols for Crosspicking Ukulele
Josef Pekárek Two Hanakian operas for Ukulele
How to play on three ukulele simultaneously
Clawhammer solo for Ukulele
Gospel Crosspicking Ukulele Solos
48 Fingerstyle Studies for Ukulele
Compositions for ukulele
18 Dance Tunes from Caslav Region for Ukulele
Francisco Tárrega for Ukulele (MB)
10 songs from the years 1899-1920 for Ukulele
Czech Hymnbook for Ukulele
Campanella style songbook for intermediate
Songs from old Prague for Ukulele
Lute music by Nicolaus Schmall von Lebendorf for Ukulele

For C tuning with low G
Irish tunes for all ukulele
Gospel Ukulele low G Solos
Antonin Dvorak: Biblical Songs: for Ukulele with low G
Gregorian chant for Ukulele with low G
The Czech Lute for Ukulele with low G
Romantic Pieces by Frantisek Max Knize for Ukulele with low G
Notebook for Anna Magdalena Bach and Ukulele with low G
Robert Burns songs for ukulele with low G
Jewish songs for ukulele with low G
Campanella style songbook for beginner: ukulele with low G
Czech Medieval Ukulele with low G
Christmas Carols for ukulele with low G
Fingerpicking solo for Ukulele with low G
43 Ghiribizzi by Niccolo Paganini for Ukulele with low G
Christmas Carols for Crosspicking Ukulele with low G
Czech Renaissance folk songs for Ukulele with low G
Gospel Crosspicking Ukulele with low G Solos
Josef Pekárek Two Hanakian operas for Ukulele with low G
18 Dance Tunes from Caslav Region for Ukulele with low G
10 songs from the years 1899-1920 for Ukulele with low G
Czech Hymnbook for Ukulele with low G
Boogie woogie patterns for ukulele with low G
Compositions for ukulele with low G
Second Fingerpicking solo for Ukulele with low G
Double Stop Gospel for Ukulele with low G
Songs from old Prague for Ukulele with low G
Lute music by Nicolaus Schmall von Lebendorf for Ukulele with low G

For Baritone ukulele
Irish tunes for all ukulele
Gospel Baritone Ukulele Solos
Antonin Dvorak: Biblical Songs: for Baritone Ukulele
Gregorian chant for Baritone Ukulele
The Czech Lute for Baritone Ukulele
Romantic Pieces by Frantisek Max Knize for Baritone Ukulele
Notebook for Anna Magdalena Bach and Baritone Ukulele
Robert Burns songs for Baritone ukulele
Jewish songs for baritone ukulele
Campanella style songbook for beginner: Baritone ukulele
Czech Medieval Baritone Ukulele
Christmas Carols for Baritone ukulele
Fingerpicking solo for Baritone ukulele
43 Ghiribizzi by Niccolo Paganini for Baritone ukulele
Christmas Carols for Crosspicking Baritone ukulele
Czech Renaissance folk songs for Baritone ukulele
Gospel Crosspicking Baritone Ukulele Solos
Josef Pekárek Two Hanakian operas for Baritone Ukulele
18 Dance Tunes from Caslav Region for Baritone Ukulele
10 songs from the years 1899-1920 for Baritone Ukulele
Czech Hymnbook for Baritone Ukulele
Boogie woogie patterns for Baritone Ukulele
Compositions for Baritone Ukulele
Second Fingerpicking solo for Baritone Ukulele
Double Stop Gospel for Baritone Ukulele
Songs from old Prague for Baritone Ukulele
Lute music by Nicolaus Schmall von Lebendorf for Baritone Ukulele

For Baritone ukulele with high D
Jewish songs for baritone ukulele with high D
Campanella style songbook for beginner Baritone ukulele with high D
Solo and Variations for Baritone ukulele with high D volume 1., 2., 3.

For 6 sting ukulele (Lili'u ukulele)
Gospel 6 string Ukulele Solos
Gregorian chant for 6 string Ukulele
Notebook for Anna Magdalena Bach and string Ukulele
Robert Burns songs for 6 string ukulele

Open G Baritone Ukulele or 5-string banjo (dgbd)
Gospel for Open G Baritone Ukulele or 5-string banjo
Jewish songs for Open G Baritone Ukulele or 5-string banjo
Robert Burns songs for Open G Baritone Ukulele or 5-string banjo

Ukulele Duets
Notebook for Anna Magdalena Bach, C tuning ukulele and C tuning ukulele (CSI)
Notebook for Anna Magdalena Bach, C tuning ukulele and Ukulele with low G (CSI)
Notebook for Anna Magdalena Bach, C tuning ukulele and Baritone ukulele (CSI)
Notebook for Anna Magdalena Bach, Ukulele with low G and Ukulele with low G (CSI)
Notebook for Anna Magdalena Bach, Ukulele with low G and Baritone ukulele (CSI)
Notebook for Anna Magdalena Bach, Baritone ukulele and Baritone ukulele (CSI)
The canons for one or two ukuleles (CSI)
Mauro Giuliani arranged for Ukulele Duet (MB)
Notebook for Anna Magdalena Bach for Ukulele and EADGBE Guitar (CSI)

New Diatonic Accordion (Melodeon) books
For G/C diatonic accordion
Bass songbook for G/C melodeon
Cross row style songbook for beginner
G/C diatonic accordion
Gospel G/C diatonic accordion Solos
9 songs from the years 1899-1920 for G/C melodeon
Czech Hymnbook for G/C melodeon
Songbook for G/C diatonic accordion *Volume 1.*
Songbook for G/C diatonic accordion *Volume 2.*
18 popular Czech Minuet for G/C diatonic accordion
Songs from old Prague for G/C diatonic accordion

For C/F diatonic accordion
Cross row style songbook for beginner
C/F diatonic accordion
Gospel C/F diatonic accordion Solos
9 songs from the years 1899-1920 for C/F melodeon

For D/G diatonic accordion
Cross row style songbook for beginner

Kalimba
Songbook for Kalimba B11 Melody
Second songbook for Kalimba B11 Melody
Songbooks for Kalimba Am+G
Czech Hymnbook for Alto *Hugh Tracey* Kalimba
Robert Burns songs for Alto *Hugh Tracey* Kalimba
Songbooks for Kalimba E116

New Flute Recorder books
18 Dance Tunes from Caslav Region for Recorder Quartet
Josef Pekárek Two Hanakian operas for Recorder Quartet

Saxophone Quartet books
18 Dance Tunes from Caslav Region for Saxophone Quartet
Josef Pekárek Two Hanakian operas for Saxophone Quartet

Notebook for Wolfgang for Ukulele and EADGBE Guitar (CSI)
For Slide ukulele (lap steel ukulele)
Comprehensive Slide Ukulele: Guidance for Slide Ukulele Playing
Gospel Slide Ukulele Solos
Irish tunes for slide ukulele
Robert Burns songs for Slide ukulele

For D tuning ukulele
Skola hry na ukulele (G+W s.r.o.)
Irish tunes for all ukulele (CSI)
Jewish songs for D tuning ukulele (CSI)
Campanella style songbook for beginner: D tuning ukulele (CSI)

For EADA tuning ukulele
EADA ukulele tuning (CSI)
Gospel EADA Ukulele Solos (CSI)

D/G diatonic accordion
Gospel D/G diatonic accordion Solos
9 songs from the years 1899-1920 for D/G melodeon

New Anglo Concertina books

For C/G 30-button Wheatstone Lachenal System
Gospel Anglo Concertina Solos (CSI)
Notebook for Anna Magdalena Bach and Anglo Concertina (CSI)
Robert Burns songs for Anglo Concertina (CSI)
The Czech Lute for Anglo Concertina (CSI)
Gregorian chant for Anglo Concertina (CSI)
Josef Pekárek *Two Hanakian operas* for Anglo Concertina (CSI)

For C/G 20-button
Gospel C/G Anglo Concertina Solos (CSI)
Robert Burns songs for C/G Anglo Concertina (CSI)
Gregorian chant for Anglo Concertina (CSI)

Songbooks for Alto *Hugh Tracey* Kalimba
Songbooks for Kalimba *Heavenly A tuning*
First Songbooks for 10 Key Kalimba
Second Songbooks for 10 Key Kalimba
Songbooks for Kalimba C diatonic tuning
Irish tunes for Alto Hugh Tracey Kalimba

Czech Medieval Songs For Two Recorders
Robert Burns songs for Recorder Quartet
Songs from old Prague for Recorder Quartet

Robert Burns songs for Saxophone Quartet
Songs from old Prague for Saxophone Quartet

Publishing House
CSI = CreateSpace Independent Publishing Platform
MB = Mel Bay Publications
G+W = G+W s.r.o.

Printed in Great Britain
by Amazon